# Samosa Recipe Book

By Brad Hoskinson

# Table of Contents

# Samosa Chaat

If you're looking for a delicious, fun and easy snack to make, you have to try samosa chaat! This dish is a twist on the classic samosa, and it's always a hit with everyone who tries it. Plus, it's really simple to make - you just need some Samosas, chickpeas, yogurt, tomatoes, and onions. Give it a try!

---

Prep Time 15 mins | Cook Time 25 mins

---

## Ingredients

### Chana Masala

- 2 tablespoon olive oil
- 1 teaspoon cumin seeds
- 2 bay leaf
- 1 cup chopped onions red or white onion
- 3 teaspoons minced ginger 1/2 inch, grated or minced
- 3 teaspoons minced garlic 2 cloves, grated or minced
- 2 tablespoon finely chopped serrano chili seeds removed for mild
- 1 cup crushed tomatoes 1 Roma tomato, pureed or finely chopped
- 1 teaspoon salt
- 1/4 teaspoon turmeric powder
- 2 teaspoon coriander powder
- 2 teaspoon garam masala
- 1 teaspoon cumin powder
- 1 teaspoon Kashmiri red chili powder or paprika, for mild
- 1 teaspoon amchur (dry mango powder) or substitute 1 teaspoon lime juice
- 1 teaspoon chaat masala or substitute 1 teaspoon lime juice
- 2 cups cooked chickpeas 2 (17 ounces) can or 3/4 cup dried & soaked (see notes 1 & 2)
- 2 cup water
- 2 tablespoons chopped cilantro for finishing

### Samosa Chaat

- 5 samosas homemade or store-bought
- 5 tablespoon tamarind chutney homemade or store-bought
- 5 tablespoons cilantro chutney homemade
- 2 pinch chaat masala
- 2 pinch roasted cumin powder
- 2 pinch cayenne optional
- 3 tablespoon thin sev (I like the Haldiram brand)
- 3 tablespoons chopped cilantro

## Instructions

### Chana Masala in Instant Pot

1. Select Saute and preheat the pressure cooker. When hot, add oil, cumin seeds, and bay leaf. When cumin seeds sizzle, add chopped onions. Saute for 5 minutes until onions soften.
2. Add minced ginger, garlic, and finely chopped serrano and saute another 3 minutes.
3. Add crushed tomato along with the spices listed for chana masala. Stir and cook for a minute.
4. Add cooked chickpeas and water.
5. Turn off Saute and scrape the bottom of the pot to remove any brown bits.
6. Close the lid and cook for 7 minutes at high pressure on sealing mode.
7. Wait 7 minutes after pressure cooking and then release the pressure manually (QR) by following the quick release instructions of your cooker. Open the lid after the pin drops. Stir and check for taste. If the curry looks thin, simmer for a few minutes on saute mode. Finish with cilantro.

### Assemble Samosa Chaat

1. Add 1 cup of cooked chana masala to a wide serving bowl.
2. Place a cooked samosa on top. You can break it up or serve it intact based on your preference.

3. Top with 4 teaspoons each of tamarind chutney and cilantro chutney.
4. Top with a pinch of chaat masala, roasted cumin, cayenne (optional), and a teaspoon of thin sev and chopped cilantro.

**Notes**

1. **Use dried chickpeas or canned**. This is more about personal preference and timing. If you use dried chickpeas, you must soak and cook 1 cup of dry chickpeas to get the same amount as 2 cans. If using canned, rinse and drain the chickpeas before cooking.
2. **One step in cooking for 'dried' chickpeas**. Simply follow the steps in the recipe card, add the chickpeas when called for and adjust the cooking times as follows:
3. **Dried and Soaked Overnight**: 50 minutes at Bean/Chili mode or Manual. Natural Pressure Release for 15 minutes, followed by Quick Release.
4. **Dried and Unsoaked:** 65 minutes at Bean/Chili mode or Manual. Natural Pressure Release for 15 minutes, followed by Quick Release.
5. **Try Dahi Samosa Chaat** by seasoning 1 cup of yogurt with salt, roasted cumin powder, cayenne, and a pinch of sugar, seasoned to your taste. Use vegan yogurt to keep the recipe completely vegan.
6. **Make ahead and store each component separately** in the fridge. The chole and samosas will keep for up to 2 days. If making the chutneys at home, they will keep well in an airtight container in the fridge for up to 1 week.
7. **Reheat the chana masala and samosas until warmed through**. For best results, reheat the chana masala in the Instant Pot on simmer mode for 25 minutes, stirring occasionally. To **reheat the samosas,** simply place them on a parchment-lined baking sheet and heat through in a 400-degree F oven for 15-20 minutes. Alternatively, heat them in a single layer in the air fryer set to ...

# Pinwheel Samosa

I know what you're thinking. Indian food? Again? But trust me, these pinwheel samosas are worth it. They're the perfect appetizer for your next party and are surprisingly easy to make. All you need is some flour, oil, and a few spices. So roll up your sleeves and let's get cooking!

Prep Time 20 mins | Cook Time 10 mins | Total Time 30 mins

## Ingredients

### Samosa Filling

- 3 gold potatoes (medium) (about 2 cups), 1 large russet potato
- 2 tablespoon avocado oil or olive oil
- 1 teaspoon cumin seeds
- 1 cup onion finely chopped, about 1/3 an onion
- 3 teaspoon jalapeno deseeded and finely chopped
- 3 teaspoon ginger finely chopped
- 1 cup frozen peas thawed
- 3 tablespoon chopped cilantro

### Spices for Samosa Filling

- 1 teaspoon salt
- 2 teaspoon ground coriander
- 3/4 teaspoon garam masala
- 3/4 teaspoon Red Chili Powder or cayenne
- 1 teaspoon amchur (dry mango powder- or 2 teaspoon lime juice)
- 1 teaspoon Chaat Masala (or 2 teaspoons lime juice)

### Pinwheels

- 2 sheets Frozen puff pastry Thawed in the refrigerator for 4-5 hours

## Instructions

**Boil Potatoes (Instant Pot or Microwave)**

1. **Instant Pot**: Place the trivet in the inner pot. Pour 2 cups water and place potatoes on the trivet. Close the lid (sealing position) and pressure cook for 7 mins at high pressure. If using russet potato, increase time to 10 mins.
2. **Microwave**: Poke potatoes with a fork. In a microwave-safe bowl, add potatoes and fill the bowl halfway through with water. Cook potatoes using the 'Potatoes preset", or for 7 mins at high temperature. Check for doneness by inserting a knife. If still not done, microwave for another 3 mins.
3. When potatoes are cool enough to handle, peel and mash them. Keep aside.

**Samosa Filling**

1. Heat a nonstick pan on medium-high heat (it takes 35-50 seconds). Add oil and cumin seeds.
2. When cumin seeds begin to sizzle, add chopped onion and jalapeno. Saute for 5 minutes. Turn off the heat.
3. Add finely chopped ginger and spices, including salt, coriander, garam masala, red chili powder, and amchur. Stir everything. The residual heat from the onions is enough to bloom the spices and ginger.
4. Add mashed potatoes and mix everything to combine. Add thawed peas and chopped cilantro. Mix well and set aside.

**Pinwheels**

1. Thaw one sheet of 'rectangle-shaped' store-bought puff pastry in the refrigerator. It should take 4 hours. Keep it refrigerated till the filling is cool and ready for use.
2. Remove the puff pastry sheet from the fridge. Sprinkle a bit of all-purpose flour on any rolling surface and rolling pin. Using the

rolling pin, thin out the pastry sheet, so it expands by 16-21% in size (roughly).

3. Using the back of a spoon or an offset spatula, spread the samosa filling in a thin layer over the pastry sheet, leaving 1/4 inch from the sides.
4. Now roll the sheet-like a log, starting from the longer side. Use smaller flips, so it rolls up into a tight log.
5. Once rolled, roll it a few times so it seems to seal tightly. Now, trim off 1/2 inch at the edges and discard. Using a sharp knife, cut the log into 1/2 inch discs. Lay the discs flat and 'gently' press down with your fingers, flattening it a bit.

## Bake it- Air fryer or oven

1. **Air Fryer:** Lay the discs down in the fryer basket, keeping a little distance between each. Air fry them at 410°F for 8 mins. Don't overcrowd the basket, as that prevents them from puffing up and getting crisp.
2. **Oven**: Lay the pinwheel discs on an aluminum or parchment-lined baking sheet, keeping a little distance between each. Bake as per the pastry-box directions. I mostly end up baking them for 12-14 in a preheated oven at 400°F.

## Serving Suggestion

Cool the pinwheels for 10-15 minutes. Then serve them with cilantro chutney and tamarind chutney, or even ketchup!

## Notes

1. Chill the samosa filling completely. If you spread warm potato filling on the cold puff pastry, it will melt the fat in the pastry, completely ruining its light, flaky texture.
2. Make sure the puff pastry remains as cold as possible. This ensures your samosa pinwheels will bake to a light and crispy texture. Follow the Tips For Working With Puff Pastry above.
3. Spread the potato filling as even as possible and leave a border. The even layer will produce an even spiral of potato filling

throughout the pastry. The border ensures the pastry rolls and seals properly. For extra insurance, you can brush a light layer of cold water on the outer edge where you will seal so the pastry sticks together.

4. Leave a generous amount of space between each pinwheel when baking - at least 3 inches. This facilitates enough air circulation around each pastry puff, promoting even cooking and that beautiful golden brown color.

5. For extra golden color, you can (optionally) brush the top of each samosa pinwheel with a light coating of egg wash (2 eggs whisked with 3 tablespoons of water).

6. Easily double the recipe. Since most puff pastry packages come with two pastry sheets, simply double the recipe and use the whole package. It's also another great way to feed a crowd!

# Samosa Recipe - Air Fryer, Fried & Baked

If you're looking for an easy and delicious Indian-inspired dish to make at home, look no further than samosas. There are a few different ways to make them, but this recipe for Air Fryer, Fried & Baked Samosas is my favorite. They're perfect for a party or as a weekday dinner meal. Give them a try!

Prep Time 35 mins | Cook Time 25 mins

### **Ingredients**

## For Samosa Dough

- 3 cups all-purpose flour (maida)
- 1 teaspoon salt
- 2 teaspoon carom seeds (ajwain)
- 6 tablespoons avocado oil
- 7 tablespoons cold water or as needed

## For Samosa Stuffing

- 2 tablespoon olive oil
- 2 teaspoon cumin seeds
- 3 teaspoons ginger finely chopped
- 2 teaspoon salt adjust to taste after cooking
- 2 teaspoon garam masala
- 2 tablespoon crushed coriander seeds or ground coriander
- 1 teaspoon red chili powder (cayenne); reduce to 1/4 teaspoon or skip for mild
- 1 teaspoon dry mango powder amchur
- 4 tablespoons water
- 4 medium gold potatoes boiled and chopped
- 2 cup green peas thawed, adjust to your liking
- 4 tablespoons cilantro finely chopped

## Oil for Air Fryer Samosa

- 4 tablespoons avocado oil to brush assembled samosas

**Oil for Deep Frying Samosas**

- 3 cups canola or vegetable oil

## Instructions

**Knead Samosa Dough**

1. Add flour, salt, and carom seeds to the food processor jar. Add oil while running the machine on low speed until the flour absorbs the oil and looks crumbly. Alternatively, add the ingredients to a large bowl, add oil and rub with your fingers till it gets crumbly.

2. To check if the dough is ready for water, press a small portion between your palm and see if it holds shape. If it falls apart, add another teaspoon of oil until it does.

3. Add water a little at a time, and knead on low speed until a firm dough is formed. Scrape the sides of the bowl halfway through. It should take around 5 minutes for the dough to come together. If kneading by hand, knead until the dough ball comes together.

4. Transfer the dough to a bowl and cover it with a damp kitchen towel to prevent it from drying and cracking. Rest it for 1.5 hours. Prepare the filling while the dough rests.

**Make the Stuffing**

1. Heat oil in a nonstick pan on medium-high heat. Add cumin seeds and saute until they sizzle. Add ginger and spices. Make sure to add 5 tablespoons of water to prevent the spices from burning. Cook for 35 seconds while stirring.

2. Stir in chopped boiled potatoes, and gently crush them using your spatula or a potato masher. Stir in peas and cook for another 3 minutes.

3. Adjust seasoning to taste. Add chopped cilantro and turn off the heat.

## Shape, Stuff and How to Fold Samosa

1. Give the dough another quick knead for 35 seconds. Now divide the dough into 8 portions and roll each into a smooth ball. Cover the dough balls with a damp kitchen towel to prevent drying.

2. Place a dough ball on a flat surface. Add a few drops of oil on each side of the dough ball and roll it into an evenly thick 6-inch disc using a rolling pin. The thickness of the dough should be about 1/16th inch.

3. Cut the disc in half to form two semi-circles. Place one semi-circle with the rounded edge facing you.

4. Apply water on the left-half straight edge of the semi-circle.

5. Lift the right edge of the semi-circle and bring it down to its center while holding it.

6. Now, bring the other edge of the semi-circle (wet side) to the center, overlapping the two edges.

7. Gently press to seal both sides together to form a cone. Pinch the tip to seal well. Hold the cone upright in your hand.

8. Add 3 tablespoons of the filling to the center.

9. Apply water on the inner side of the open edges of the cone. Holding from the middle, gently bring the open seams towards the center, pinching them together to seal them.

10. Ensure that the samosa is sealed all the way through. Form all samosas using this method.

## Cook the Samosa - Air Fryer Samosa

1. Using a pastry brush, coat the samosa generously with oil. Preheat the air fryer at 395°F for 3 minutes.

2. Place the samosas in the fryer basket in a single layer, leaving about 1-inch space between each.

3. Air fry at 395°F for 15 mins. Remove the basket, flip the samosas, brush them with oil and cook them for another 15 minutes. After that, remove the basket, brush the samosas lightly with oil, increase the temperature to 450°F and air fry for 3 minutes.

## Fried Samosa on the Stovetop

1. Heat 3 cups canola or vegetable oil in a heavy bottom wok on medium-low heat for about 20 minutes. To confirm if the oil is at the right temperature, drop a small crumble of the dough into the oil. The oil is ready if multiple tiny bubbles start forming around the dough. If it floats to the top immediately, reduce the heat and wait for the oil to cool down.

2. Place a samosa on the spoon and carefully slide it into the hot oil. Repeat with 3 more samosas without overcrowding the wok. Fry for about 17-20 minutes on medium-low heat, flipping 2-3 times until the samosa turns golden in color.

Remove samosas and transfer on onto a kitchen towel-lined plate to absorb the excess oil. Fry the remaining samosas by following this process.

## Oven-Baked Samosa

Preheat the oven to 395°F. Line a baking sheet with aluminum foil. Brush the samosas generously with oil. Place the samosas on the baking sheet, leaving about 1-inch space between each. Bake for 30-35 minutes. After about 20 minutes, flip them and brush with a little more oil. Bake until golden brown.

## Notes:

## Dough Making Tips:

1. After adding oil to the dough, mix it until it resembles coarse sand. To check if it's ready for water, press it together between your palm and see if it holds shape. If it falls apart, add another teaspoon of oil until it does. This step is called 'moyen or moyan' in Hindi.

2. Add cold water to make the dough to achieve a crisp crust.

3. Rest the dough for one hour. I tried two batches with a rest time of 30 minutes and 45 minutes, respectively, and both didn't work as well as the dough that was rested for an hour.

4. Cover the dough with a wet kitchen towel while resting to prevent it from drying and cracking.

## Rolling Tips:

1. For a smoother rolling experience, add a few drops of oil to the dough ball before you start rolling.

2. Roll on a wooden cutting board instead of a smooth countertop. The added texture in the wooden board makes rolling this stretchy dough easier.

3. Roll them evenly. Roll the dough into an even thickness to ensure even cooking and crisping. The shape should be round or oval. Don't worry if it's not a perfect circle.

## Samosa Folding Tips:

1. When using water to seal the edges, use very little. Excess water can make it harder to seal.

2. When overlapping the two rounded edges, make sure to overlap at least 1/2-inch. That prevents the dough from opening when frying or air frying.

3. Use cooled filling to stuff the samosas. A warm filling will loosen the fat in the dough and prevent it from crisping up.

## Samosa Cooking Tips:

1. If deep-frying, perform the dough test mentioned in the recipe steps to ensure that the oil is at the right temperature for deep frying. If the oil is too hot, samosas will brown while being undercooked on the inside. If the oil is too cold, it will absorb excess oil and be greasy.

2. Brush liberally with oil for air frying. To get a crisp crust, brush the samosas generously with oil before adding them to the air fryer and halfway through after flipping them.

# Samosa Stuffed Jalapeno Poppers

If you love Indian food, you'll love these jalapeno poppers. Samosas are a popular Indian dish made by stuffing a savory filling inside a crispy pastry shell. This recipe uses samosa filling to stuff jalapeno peppers instead of the traditional bread dough. The result is a delicious appetizer that is sure to impress your guests!

Prep Time 20 mins | Cook Time 10 mins | Total Time 30 mins

### Ingredients

- 7 Jalapeno Chili cut in half lengthwise and deseeded

**Samosa Filling**

- 3 gold potatoes (medium) (about 2cups), 1 large russet potato
- 2 tbsp avocado oil or olive oil
- 1 tsp cumin seeds
- 1 cup onion finely chopped, about ⅓ an onion
- 3 tsp jalapeno deseeded and finely chopped
- 3 tsp ginger finely chopped
- 3/4 cup frozen peas thawed
- 3 tbsp chopped cilantro

**Spices for Samosa Filling**

- 1 tsp salt
- 2 tsp ground coriander
- 3/4 tsp garam masala
- 3/4 tsp Red Chili Powder or cayenne
- 1 tsp amchur (dry mango powder)(see notes for substitute)
- 1 tsp Chaat Masala

**Garnish**

- Cilantro Chutney
- Tamarind Chutney

## Instructions

### Boil Potatoes (Instant Pot or Microwave)

1. Instant Pot: Place the trivet in the inner pot. Pour 1 cup of water and place potatoes on the trivet. Close the lid (sealing position) and pressure cook for 10 mins at HIGH pressure. If using russet potato, increase time to 10 mins.
2. Microwave: Poke potatoes with a fork. In a microwave-safe bowl, add potatoes and fill the bowl halfway through with water. Cook potatoes using the 'Potatoes preset", or for 10 mins at HIGH temperature. Check for doneness. If still not done, microwave for another 5 mins.
3. When potatoes are cool enough to handle, peel and mash them. Keep aside.

### Samosa Filling

1. Heat a nonstick pan on medium-high heat (it takes 35-50 seconds). Add oil and cumin seeds.
2. When cumin seeds begin to sizzle, add chopped onion and jalapeno. Saute for 5 minutes. Turn off the heat.
3. Add finely chopped ginger and spices, including salt, coriander, garam masala, red chili powder, and amchur. Stir everything. The residual heat from the onions is enough to bloom the spices and ginger.
4. Add mashed potatoes and mix everything to combine. Add thawed peas and chopped cilantro. Mix well and set aside.

### Stuff and Bake Jalapeños

1. Wash and dry jalapeños peppers. Cut off the stem end, then cut in half lengthwise. Using a spoon, scrape off the seeds and membrane in each.
2. Toss them in a teaspoon of avocado (or olive) oil and a few dashes of salt and pepper.
3. Fill each jalapeño half with 3 teaspoons of samosa filling and bake them using one of the following three ways:

4. Air Fryer: Brush the fry basket with avocado oil or lightly spray with a cooking spray. Place the stuffed jalapeños in the basket, leaving a little space between each. Cook at 420°F for 8 minutes. After 10 mins, the jalapeño will be al dente in texture, which means they'll have a little crunch. If you like them softer, increase the air frying time to 15 mins.
5. Crisplid: Brush the mesh basket with oil or spray with cooking spray. Place trivet in the inner steel pot of Instant Pot or Multipot, then place the mesh basket on that. Place the stuffed jalapeños in the basket, leaving a little space between each. Cook at 420°F for 10 minutes.
6. Oven: Line a baking sheet with aluminum foil (the heat transferred from the aluminum foil helps the peppers cook faster). Place the stuffed jalapeños leaving a little space between each. Bake at 420°F for 15-17 minutes.

## Garnish

Garnish each stuffed jalapeño with about 3/4 teaspoon of cilantro and tamarind chutney! These Samosa Stuffed jalapeño poppers are best served warm.

## Notes:

**Recipe Tips for Samosa Stuffed Jalapeno Poppers:**

- Scrape off the seeds and membrane in each pepper. This will tone down the spice factor in the peppers and allow you to taste more of the samosa filling. And don't forget to wear gloves!
- Bake to your desired tenderness. I enjoy these spicy peppers al dente or with a bit of crunch left in the peppers. If you like your jalapenos soft, add 3 minutes to the baking method.
- Serve warm. Jalapenos taste best when they are still slightly warm, so bake these just before your guests arrive, garnish and transfer to a serving platter.

# Mutter & Asparagus Samosa

Mutter & Asparagus Samosa is a great dish to prepare when you have guests coming over. It's really easy to make and looks impressive. Plus, it's a lot healthier than your average party appetizer. Give it a try!

Prep Time: 25 minutes Cook Time: 20 minutes Total Time40: Indian

## Ingredients

- 7 samosa patties
- 3 tbsp plain flour (maida) dissolved with 3 tbsp water
- oil for deep-frying

### For The Filling

- 1  cup boiled green peas- half mashed
- 1 cup fresh asparagus (cut into cubes &boiled) or canned mashed
- 1 cup sweet potato – boiled, peeled and mashed
- 2 tsp oil
- 3/4 tsp carom seeds (ajwain)
- 1 inch. Grated ginger
- 3 tsp green chili paste
- 3 tsp lemon juice
- 2 tsp sugar
- 3/4 tsp garam masala
- salt to taste

## Process

### For the filling

1. Heat the oil in a nonstick pan and add the carom seeds, grated ginger, green chili paste, green peas, and asparagus, and sauté on a medium flame for 3 minutes.
2. Add the sugar, mashed sweet potatoes, garam masala, and salt, mix well and cook on a medium flame for 1 minute. Remove from flame and add lemon juice.

3. Divide the filling into 7 equal portions and keep aside.

**For the samosas**

1. Fold the right bottom corner (right angle) of the samosa Patti on the opposite side to form a triangle.
2. Fold the entire triangle towards its left and fold diagonally on the opposite side to make a cone.
3. Fill a portion of the filling and seal the edges using the maida-water paste, so the filling does not spill out.
4. Repeat these same steps to make 5 more samosas.
5. Heat the oil in a deep nonstick kadhai and deep-fry a few samosas on a slow flame until they turn golden brown in color from all sides. Drain on absorbent paper.
6. Serve hot

# Samosa Chaat - Easy Mini Samosa Recipe

Are you looking for an easy samosa recipe? This one is perfect for a quick snack or appetizer. Samosa chaat is a delicious combination of mini samosas and chutney. It's simple to make and sure to please your taste buds. Give it a try today!

Prep Time: 15-20 minutes Cook Time: 35-40 minutes Total Time 50-55 minutes

## Ingredients

### For Samosa Filling

- 4 tbsp Ghee
- 3 green chili, chopped
- 1 inch Ginger, chopped
- 3 cups Green peas
- Salt to taste
- 3/4 cup fresh Mint leaves, chopped
- little Water
- 1 tsp Sugar
- 2 tsp Ghee
- 3/4 inch Ginger, chopped
- few mint leaves, chopped
- 2 green chili, chopped
- 1 tbsp Prepared Chaat Masala

### For Tamarind Chutney

- 2 liter Water
- 2 cups tamarind, soaked
- 3 cups jaggery

### For Tempering Chutney

- 2 tbsp Oil
- 3 Cloves

- 2 tsp Cumin seeds
- 3 dry Red chilies
- 2 tsp Degi red chili powder
- A pinch of asafoetida

## For Chaat Masala

- 3 tbsp Black peppercorns
- 2 tbsp Coriander seed
- 2 tbsp Fennel seed
- 2 no Black cardamom seeds
- 1 tbsp Cumin seeds
- Salt to taste

## For Dough

- 2 cups Refined flour
- 1 tsp Carom seeds, crushed
- Salt to taste
- 2 tbsp Ghee
- chilled water as required

## Other Ingredients

- Oil for frying

## For Masala

- 2 tbsp Ghee
- 4 green chili, slit into half
- Salt to taste
- 1 inch Ginger, julienned
- 3/4 cup Prepared Samosa Filling
- little water
- 2 tsp Prepared Chaat masala

## For Garnish

- Prepared Masala

- Curd, beaten and seasoned
- Prepared Samosa
- Prepared Tamarind chutney
- Curd, beaten and seasoned
- Pomegranate pearl
- Sev
- few Coriander sprig
- A pinch of Prepared chaat masala

## Process

### For Samosa Filling

1. Take a shallow pan or Kadai, add ghee once it's hot, add green chili, ginger, and mint leaves and saute it well. Add green peas and salt to taste and saute it well. Cover it with the lid and cook for 5 minutes on medium flame.
2. Once the green peas are cooked, add a little water and mix it well.
3. Once again, cover it with a lid and cook for a while. Open the lid. Once the green peas are cooked well, mash the green peas, add sugar and saute for a minute.
4. Now, add ghee and saute once again. Switch off the flame, add ginger, mint leaves, and green chili and mix well.
5. Transfer the prepared filling to the plate or tray and keep it in the refrigerator for a while.

### For Tamarind Chutney

Add water, tamarind, and jaggery to a saucepot, cover it with a lid, and cook for 20 to 25 minutes. Once the chutney is cooked well, strain the mixture and keep it aside for further use.

### For Tempering Chutney

1. In a handi, add oil. Once the oil is hot, add cloves and let it splutter well.
2. Add cumin seeds, dry red chili, and let them splutter well.

3. Pour the prepared chutney and mix properly. Add degi red chili powder and asafoetida and mix well.
4. Cook on medium heat for 15-20 minutes. Once the chutney gets thickened nicely.
5. Transfer into the bowl and keep aside for further use.

## For Chaat Masala

1. Add black peppercorns, coriander seed, black cardamom seed, fennel seed, cumin seeds, and salt to taste in a bowl.
2. Transfer into a pan and dry roast the spices on medium flame. Once it cools down, transfer it into a grinder and grind it coarsely. Keep it aside for future use.

## For Dough

1. In a parat, add refined flour, carom seeds, salt to taste, and ghee. Mix everything properly until it resembles bread crumbs.
2. Now, add chilled water and knead a hard dough. Cover and keep aside for resting at least for 15-20 minutes.

## For Assembling

1. Take a medium portion of the dough, make a round peda, apply ghee and roll it thin in an oval shape.
2. Now, cut in from the center, take one half of it, make a cone shape, and add the prepared filling.
3. Now apply water to the open ends of the cone and fold it towards you. Keep it down, give it a gentle press so it can stand, and make all others similar.
4. Heat oil in a kadhai on medium heat and fry the samosas on low to medium heat until it turns golden in color from all the sides; remove on an absorbent paper.

## For Masala

1. Add ghee to a pan. Once the ghee is hot, add green chili and ginger and saute them well.
2. Add prepared samosa filling and salt to taste and mix well.

3.  Add little water, prepare chaat masala and mix them nicely and keep it aside for further use.

**For Garnish**

On a serving plate, place the prepared masala, seasoned curd, samosa, curd, tamarind chutney, ready chaat masala, pomegranate pearl, sprinkle sev, coriander sprig, and serve hot.

# Famous Pinwheel Samosa Recipe

Do you love samosas? If so, this is the perfect recipe for you! Famous Pinwheel Samosas are a delicious and easy-to-make snack that everyone will enjoy. They're perfect for parties or any other special occasion. Try them out today!

Prep Time: 15-20 minutes | Cook Time: 25-30 minutes | Total Time 35-45 minutes

## Ingredients

**For Masala**

- 2 tbsp Coriander seeds
- 1 tbsp Cumin seeds
- 2 tbsp Fennel seeds
- 2 tbsp Black peppercorns
- 2 Black cardamom seeds

**For Filling**

- 2 tbsp Oil
- 3/4 tsp Cumin seeds
- 2 inch Ginger, chopped
- 3 fresh green chilies, chopped
- 5 medium-size potatoes, boiled & slightly mashed
- Salt to taste
- 2 tbsp Prepared Masala
- 3/4 tsp Sugar
- 3/4 tsp Dry Mango powder
- 2 tbsp Coriander leaves, chopped

**For Dough**

- 2 cups Refined flour
- 3/4 tsp Carom seeds
- Salt to taste

- 3 tsp Ghee
- Water as required
- Oil to deep-fry

## For Garnish

- Tomato ketchup
- Green chutney
- Coriander sprig
- Lemon wedge

## Process

### For Masala

- In a pan, add coriander seeds, cumin seeds, fennel seeds, black peppercorns, and black cardamom seeds, and dry roast on medium flame.
- Transfer it into a bowl, and add salt to taste once it cools completely.
- Transfer it into a grinder jar and grid it coarsely.
- Keep it aside for further use.

### For Filling

- Heat oil in a pan, add cumin seeds and let it splutter well.
- Add ginger and green chili and saute it well.
- Add mashed boiled potatoes and mix them well.
- Add salt to taste, prepare masala and mix everything well.
- Add sugar, and dry mango powder and mix it well.
- Add coriander leaves and mix it well. Transfer it into a bowl and keep it aside for further use.

### For Dough

- In a parat, add refined flour, carom seeds, salt to taste, ghee and water and knead a semi-soft dough.
- Cover it with a damp cloth and rest for 15 minutes.

**For Frying**

- Dust the dough with refined flour and roll the dough with a rolling pin into a rectangle shape.
- Now, spread the prepared potato filling evenly, apply little water and slightly press.
- Roll tight to make sure the stuffing is intact. Use a little water to seal the end of the sheet firmly.
- Keep in a refrigerator for 15 minutes so that it holds its shape.
- Once it holds the shape. Cut the roll to a half-inch slice and flatten slightly.
- Heat oil in a Kadai deep-fries the pinwheels until both sides are golden-brown.
- Keep the flame on low to medium and stir occasionally.
- Remove on an absorbent paper.
- Garnish it with a coriander sprig and lemon wedge.
- Finally, serve pinwheel samosa with green chutney and tamarind chutney.

# Keema Samosa

I hope everyone is having a great weekend. Today, I wanted to share with you a recipe for Keema Samosa. Keema Samosa is an Indian dish made with ground beef and potatoes. It's very easy to make and it's really delicious. I think you'll enjoy it!

Prep Time: 15-20 minutes | Cook Time: 25-30 minutes | Total Time 35-45 minutes

## Ingredients

### For Crushed Paste

- 2-inch Ginger
- 6 large Garlic cloves
- 4 fresh green chilies
- Sal to taste

### For Keema Stuffing

- 1 kg Mutton mince (keema)
- 3 tbsp Curd, beaten
- 2 Black cardamom
- 1 tsp Turmeric powder
- 2 heaped tsp Coriander powder
- 3/4 tsp Cumin powder
- 2 tsp Degi red chili powder
- 3 tsp Ghee
- 2 medium Onion, chopped
- Few Mint leaves, chopped
- Few Coriander leaves, chopped

### For Dough

- 2 cups Refined flour
- 3 tsp Ghee
- Salt to taste

- 2 whole Egg
- 1 tsp Ghee at the end
- Oil for frying

## For Smoke

- Coconut husk or coal
- 3 Cloves
- 2 tsp Ghee

## For Garnish

- Onion rings
- Fresh Mint sprig
- Coriander sprig
- Lemon wedge

## Process

### For Crushed Paste

In a mortar pestle, add ginger, garlic, green chili, and salt to taste and make a smooth paste.

### For Keema Stuffing

- Add mutton mince, curd, black cardamom, turmeric powder, coriander powder, cumin powder, degi red chili powder, and ghee; mix everything well in a medium-sized bowl.
- Transfer the keema mixture to a heavy bottom pan and saute on medium flame.
- Keep sauteing for 5 minutes, breaking the lumps, if any.
- Once the keem is cooked correctly.
- Make a well in the center of the mixture and keep a small steel Katori with a few hot charcoal pieces or coconut husk. Keep a few cloves over the coals, drizzle ghee over, and cover immediately tolet the smoky flavor infuse for 1-2 minutes. Remove the cover, remove the katori and mix the mutton mixture well. Remove the black cardamom from the mixture.

- Transfer the prepared stuffing into a bowl, add chopped onion, mint leaves, and coriander leaves, and mix it well. Let it cool down to room temperature.

## For Dough

- Add refined flour, ghee, and salt to taste in a bowl, and a whole egg kneads a firm dough.
- Cover it with a dam cloth and rest for 15-20 minutes.
- Pinch a large ball from the dough and roll out as thin as possible on a dusted floor.
- Cut into half and fold one end to make a cone, stuff it with some prepared mixture, and fold the other end over to close the open end. Apply a little water to the open edge and press to seal.
- Similarly, make more samosas with the rest of the dough and filling.

## For Frying

- Heat oil in a Kadai.
- Slide the samosas into the hot oil and deep-fry till golden brown and crisp. Drain on absorbent paper.
- Arrange them on a serving plate and serve hot with mint chutney, onion rings, lemon wedges, and mint sprigs.

# Chapati Samosa

Chapati samosa is a delicious and healthy Indian dish perfect for a quick and easy weeknight meal. This dish is made with homemade chapati dough stuffed with spicy potato masala. It's the perfect blend of Indian and Pakistani flavors, and it's sure to please everyone in your family!

Prep Time: 15 minutes | Cook Time: 30 minutes | Total Time 40 minutes

## Ingredients

- 6 leftover Chapatis
- Thick Maida slurry

**For Samosa Filling**

- 3 tbsp Oil
- 1 tsp Cumin Seeds
- 3/4 tsp Fennel seeds
- 2-inch ginger – chopped
- 2 fresh Green Chili – chopped
- 3/4 tsp Asafoetida
- 1 tsp Turmeric Powder
- 1 tsp Coriander Powder
- 4 medium Potatoes – boiled & diced
- Salt to taste

**For Garnish**

- Fresh Coriander Leaves

## Process

**For Samosa Filling**

Add oil, cumin seeds, fennel seeds, ginger, green chilies, asafoetida, turmeric powder, and coriander powder in a hot pan and mix everything properly. Switch off the flames, add the boiled potatoes salt, mix it properly, and mash it little. Keep aside for further use.

## For Chapati Samosa

- Take the leftover chapatis and cut them in half.
- Now take one-half of the chapati, apply the maida slurry to the straight end, and make a cone shape by sticking it.
- Now add the filling and apply the maida slurry to the open ends, close it properly, and add a clove to keep it together.
- Fry in medium hot oil until golden brown and crispy.
- Serving hot

# Crispy Punjabi Samosa

Samosas, a crispy, triangular-shaped Indian snack, are famous worldwide. There are many different ways to prepare them, but this recipe for Punjabi samosas is our family favorite. These samosas are stuffed with a spicy potato mixture and fried until golden brown. Serve them with chutney or dipping sauce for a delicious appetizer or snack!

Prep Time: 15 minutes | Cook Time: 30 minutes | Total Time 40 minutes

## Ingredients

**For Dough**

- 2 cup Maida
- Salt to taste
- 1 tsp Carom seeds
- 3 tbsp Ghee
- Cold water as required
- For Samosa Masala
- 2 tbsp Coriander seeds
- 2 tbsp Fennel seeds
- 1 tbsp Cumin seeds

**For Samosa Filling**

- 2 tbsp Ghee
- 2 inch Ginger, chopped
- 3 fresh green chilies, chopped
- 12-14 Raisins
- 2 tsp Turmeric powder
- 1 tsp Degi red chili powder
- 3/4 tsp Asafoetida
- 6-7 Potatoes, boiled & slightly mashed
- 3/4 cup Green peas
- 2 tbsp Prepared Masala

- 1 tsp Black pepper powder
- 2 tsp Dry Mango powder
- Salt to taste

## Process

### For Dough

- Add maida, salt, carom seeds, and ghee to a bowl and mix everything properly until it resembles bread crumbs.
- Now add cold water and knead a hard dough. Cover and keep aside for resting at least for 15-20 minutes.

### For Samosa Masala -

- In a pan, add coriander, cumin, and fennel seeds and roast them lightly.
- Transfer them into a motor-pastel, crush them coarsely, and keep them aside for further use.

### For Samosa Filling

- Add ghee, ginger, garlic, and green chilies to a pan and saute for a minute.
- Add raisins, turmeric powder, degi red chili powder, asafoetida, potatoes, and green peas, and mash it coarsely. Mix everything properly, cover, and cook for 5-7 minutes on medium heat.
- Remove the cover and cook on high flames for 5 minutes or until lightly charred.
- Add the prepared masala, black pepper powder, dry mango powder, and salt and mix everything properly. And keep them aside for further use.

### For Assembling Samosa.

- Take a medium portion of the dough, make a round peda and roll it thin in an oval shape.
- Now cut in from the center, take one half of it, make a cone shape, and add the filling.

- Now apply water on the open ends of the cone and fold it towards you; keep it down and give it a gentle press so that it can stand, similarly make all others.
- Heat oil in a kadhai on medium heat and fry the samosas until golden brown from all sides, and remove them on an absorbent paper. Serve hot with tomato ketchup.

# Chinese Samosa - Bread Samosa Crispy Vegetable Samosa

If you're looking for a new and exciting dinnertime dish, look no further than Chinese samosas! These crispy, savory rolls are stuffed with vegetables and make a delicious appetizer or main course. They're perfect for any occasion - from a casual weeknight meal to a party appetizer. So give this unique dish a try today!

Prep Time: 15 minutes | Cook Time: 20 minutes | Total Time 30 minutes

## <u>Ingredients</u>

### For filling

- 3 tbsp Oil
- 3 Spring onion white part, sliced
- 3 green chilies, sliced
- 2 inch Ginger, sliced
- 2 medium Carrot, Peeled, julienned
- 1 medium cabbage, batons
- 2 tbsp Soya sauce
- 2 tbsp Vinegar
- 2 tsp Sugar
- 3/4 cup Bread slice sides, chopped
- 4 tbsp fresh Coriander leaves with tender stem, chopped
- 2 tbsp Spring onion green part, chopped

### For cover

- 9 Bread slices, sides cut

## Process

**For filling**

- In a pan, let it heat properly, add spring onion white part, green chilies, and ginger, and saute for a minute.
- Now add carrot and cabbage, saute for 3 minutes, add soya sauce, vinegar, and sugar and mix it well.
- Once the veggies start sweating, add the bread sides and saute for 3 minutes.
- Remove from the flames, add coriander leaves and spring onion, mix everything properly, and keep aside to cool down.

**For cover and frying**

- Take a slice of bread, flatten it out with the rolling pin, and then apply very little water to it.
- Keep the filling in the center and fold it in a triangle, then seal the edges and trim the access.
- Repeat and make the rest of them. Add the prepaid samosas to medium hot oil and fry until golden brown from all sides.
- Serving hot with chai and tomato ketchup.

# Easy Samosa Recipe

I'm always looking for new and easy recipes to add to my rotation, and this samosa recipe is a winner. They're simple to make and so delicious. Plus, they're perfect for parties or potlucks. I can't wait to try them out!

Prep Time: 20-25 minutes | Cook Time: 1-30 minutes | Total Time50-55 minutes

## Ingredients

### For Dough

- 2 cups refined flour
- 1 tsp carom seeds
- 2 tbsp ghee
- Salt to taste
- Chilled water as required (Stiff dough)

### For Filling

- 4 tbsp oil
- 6 medium potatoes, boiled
- 2 tbsp ginger, finely chopped
- 2 tsp fennel seeds
- 2 tsp crushed coriander
- 1 tsp cumin seeds
- 3/4 tsp carom seeds (ajwain)
- Black pepper powder to taste
- Salt to taste
- 3/4 tsp dried mango powder (amchur powder)
- Oil for frying

## Process

### For Dough

- Add refined flour, carom seeds and ghee to a bowl, combine well with fingertips till it looks like bread crumbs.

- Add salt and mix well. Add chilled water and knead enough to combine and form a tight dough.

## For Filling

- Heat oil in a pan, ginger, fennel seeds, crushed coriander, and cumin seeds. Cook till fragrant.
- Add carom seeds and mix well. Chop the potatoes and add in, mix and cook for 7 minutes.
- Add black pepper powder, enough for taste and color both.
- Add salt and mix well. Add dried mango powder to the end and mix well.
- Allow to cool down.

## For Samosa

- Divide the prepared dough into equal portions, and roll it in an oval and long shape.
- Divide the rolled dough sheet into two halves, and shape it into a triangle forming a cone.
- Fill the dough cone with the prepared potato filling and seal the edges by overlapping them.
- Deep fry the prepared samosas in medium hot oil till golden brown and crispy.
- Drain on absorbent paper and serve hot with a choice of chutney.

# Baked Chinese Patti Samosa

Samosa is a popular Indian dish usually made with potatoes, peas, and spices. It can be fried or baked, and it's delicious no matter how you make it. In this blog post, I will show you how to make a baked Chinese Patti samosa. This variation of the traditional dish is made with ground beef, carrots, and green onions. It's still just as tasty as the original, and it's a great alternative if you want something different. So let's get started!

> Prep Time: 20 minutes | Cook Time: 30 minutes | Total Time 45 minutes

## Ingredients

**For stuffing**

- 2 tbsp olive oil
- 3 cups cabbage, shredded
- 2 cups onion, sliced
- 2 cup bean sprout
- 2 tbsp light soy sauce
- 2 tbsp red chili sauce
- salt to taste
- 1 tsp crushed black pepper
- 2 tsp sugar
- 2 tbsp corn flour,

## Other Ingredients

- Maida paste for binding samosas
- Ready-made samosa Patti
- Olive oil to brush samosas
- Ketchup to serve

## Process

- Heat olive oil and saute onion, cabbage, and bean sprout for 2-minutes on medium heat.
- Add light soy sauce, chili sauce, salt, crushed pepper, and sugar.

- When the mixture is cooked, then add corn flour and stir well. Remove from the heat and allow it to cool.
- Put tbsp of mixture on samosa Patti and bind it with maida and water pastre.
- Arrange them on a greased baking tray. Brush them with oil.
- Bake them in preheated oven at 250*C for 20 mins.
- Remove & serve hot immediately with ketchup.

# Chicken & Olive Samosa

Have you ever had a samosa? They're this delicious Indian dish made with a crispy shell filled with all sorts of goodness. Today, I'm going to show you how to make your own chicken & olive samosas. They're the perfect appetizer for any party! Enjoy!

Prep Time: 10 minutes | Cook Time: 20 minutes | Total Time 25 minutes

## Ingredients

### For the Dough

- 550g Refined Flour
- 1 tsp cumin seeds
- A pinch of salt
- 3 tbsp olive oil
- 200ml water

### For the stuffing

- 3 tbsp olive oil
- 9 pitted black olives, sliced
- 550g chicken, minced
- 2 tsp cumin seeds
- 1 tsp chili powder
- 2 tsp ginger, peeled and grated
- 2 green chili, deseeded and chopped
- Juice of 1 lime
- 3 tbsp chopped fresh coriander
- 1 cups peas, boiled
- 3/4 cup cashew nuts, chopped

## Process

- To make the dough, place the flour, cumin seeds, and a pinch of salt in a bowl. Mix the oil and water, then stir into the flour to make a soft dough. Knead for a few minutes until smooth. Return to the bowl, cover and set aside while preparing the filling.

- For the filling: heat the and add cumin seeds; when crackling, add the ginger, green chili, and onion and stir for 30 seconds. Add the olives and ground chicken and mix well; sauté for 5 mins until hot. Stir in the rest of the ingredients (green peas, coriander leaves, lime, and broken cashew nuts), stir for 2 more minutes and remove from the heat. Add salt to taste.
- Divide the dough into 8 portions. Roll and add the required quantity of the filling. Shape it like a samosa triangle.
- Deep-fry the samosas a few times in the hot Bertolli Extra Light Olive oil until golden brown. Drain on kitchen paper and serve warm with chutney.

# Keema Samosa

Have you ever tried Keema Samosa? They are a delicious Indian dish made from minced meat wrapped in a crispy pastry pocket. If you're looking for an easy way to impress your friends and family, this recipe is for you! Keema Samosas can be prepared in advance and baked when you're ready to eat them. Let's get started!

Prep Time: 25 minutes | Cook Time: 40 minutes

## Ingredients

### For Filling

- 300 gms Mutton Keema
- 2 tbsp Oil
- 3 nos. Bay leaves
- 2 medium Onion, finely chopped
- 2 tsp Ginger Garlic Paste
- 2 tsp Green Chilies, chopped
- 2 tsp Garam Masala Powder
- 3 tsp Curd
- 2 tbsp Fresh Coriander, chopped
- 2 tbsp Mint Leaves, chopped

### Other Ingredients

- 15 Samosa Patti
- Oil for deep frying

## Process

- Wash the mutton keema and let all the water drain off. Keep aside.
- Heat oil in a pan. Add bay leaves and stir for a few seconds.
- Add onion and saute for a minute. Stir in ginger garlic paste and green chilies. Cook until aroma comes out.
- Now add in the keema and saute for a minute.
- Now add garam masala powder, curd and season with salt.

- Mix everything well, cover and cook for 15 mins.
- Remove the lid and mix in the chopped coriander and mint leaves. Turn off the flame. Allow it to cool.
- Now take samosa Patti, put some mixture and fold according to the packet's instructions.
- In hot oil, deep fry the samosas till golden in color. Make sure to keep the flame low throughout cooking. Remove on absorbent paper and drain off the excess oil.
- Alternatively, you can brush some oil on the samosas and bake them in the oven at 160*c for 10-15 mins, filling mid-way.
- Serve hot with chutney.

# Mathri Recipe

Mathri is a traditional and trendy Indian savory snack. This recipe is easy to make and hearty enough to serve as a light meal. Mathri is perfect for packing your lunch or enjoying an after-school snack. Give this recipe a try today!

Prep Time: 15-20 minutes | Cook Time: 20-25 minutes | Total Time 30-40 minutes

## Ingredients

### For Chapati Dough

- 2 cups Whole wheat flour
- Salt to taste
- 3/4 cup Water
- 2 tsp Ghee

### For Paratha Dough

- 2 cups Whole wheat flour
- Salt to taste
- 1 tsp Ghee
- A pinch of Carom seeds
- 3/4 cup Water
- 2 tsp Ghee

### For Papdi Dough

- 2 cups Refined flour
- 3/4 cup Whole wheat flour
- Salt to taste
- A pinch of Black pepper powder
- A pinch of Carom seeds
- 3 tsp Ghee
- 3/4 cup Cold water
- For Ghee Mixture

- 3 tbsp Ghee
- 3 tbsp Refined flour

## For Mathri Dough

- 2 cups Refined flour
- 3/4 cup Whole wheat flour
- 2 tbsp Semolina, fine grind
- 2 tsp Gram flour
- 1 tsp Black peppercorns, crushed
- 3 tbsp Ghee
- 3/4 cup Cold water

## Other Ingredients

- 5 Black peppercorns

## Process

## For Chapati Dough

1. In a parat, add whole wheat flour, salt to taste, water, and knead a semi-soft dough
2. Apply ghee and knead it again. Cover the dough with a damp cloth and rest for 5 minutes.

## For Paratha Dough

1. In a parat, add whole wheat flour, salt to taste, ghee and carom seeds.
2. Add water little by little and knead a stiff dough.
3. Cover the dough with a damp cloth and rest for 10 minutes.

## For Samosa Dough

1. In a parat, add refined flour, whole wheat flour, salt to taste, black pepper powder, carom seeds, and ghee.
2. Add cold water little by little and knead a smooth and tight dough. Once kneaded, keep the dough aside to rest for 15 min.

3. Now roll the dough to an oval shape, apply the ghee mixture, roll it like a pinwheel, and then cut it into a small portion.
4. Take one of the portions and gently roll it using a rolling pin to a slightly thick puri.
5. Spread ghee mixture and fold half. Again spread ghee and fold the triangle.
6. Roll gently to flatten the layers.
7. Prick a black peppercorn making sure all layers are intact.
8. Drop the puri in medium hot oil.
9. Fry on low flame, occasionally stirring, for 20 minutes.
10. Keep the flame on low fry until the puri turns golden and crisp.
11. Drain off the puri, taking off excess oil.
12. Serve warm or store in an airtight container.

## For Mathri Dough

1. In a parat, add refined flour, whole wheat flour, semolina, gram flour, black peppercorns, and ghee and mix everything until it resembles bread crumb consistency.
2. Now add some water and knead a semi-hard dough. Cover and keep aside for 15-20 minutes.

# Baked Samosa

Do you love samosas? I know I do. They are one of my favorite Indian dishes. And they're not hard to make at home—they're pretty easy. You just need a few simple ingredients and a little time in the kitchen. So if you're looking for a fun and tasty dinner idea, give baked samosas a try!

---

Prep Time: 10 minutes | Cook Time: 20 minutes | Total Time: 35 minutes

---

## Ingredients

**For making Baked samosa dough**

- 2 cup flour/Maida
- Salt to taste
- 3 tbsp oil

**For Veggie Samosa Filling**

- 150 gm Paneer
- 1 cup cabbage chopped
- 1 cup boiled rajma
- 50 gm grated cheese
- 40 gm cherry tomatoes
- 2 tsp Red chili flakes
- 2 tsp peri masala

## Instructions

**To make samosa wrappers:**

1. Combine 2 cups flour, salt to taste, ajwain, and 3 tablespoons oil. Mix them well and make a stiff dough by adding cold water. Rest the dough for 35 minutes.
2. To make wrappers for Baked Samosa
3. Combine 2 cups flour, salt to taste, ajwain, and 3 tablespoons oil. Mix them well and make a stiff dough by adding cold water. Rest the dough for 35 minutes.

## Samosa Stuffing

Mix together small chopped paneer, cabbage, boiled Rajma, grated cheese, cherry tomatoes, salt to taste, red chili flakes, peri-peri masala, and a tablespoon of mayonnaise. Combine them to make samosa stuffing and keep them aside.

## To shape samosa

1. Now, divide the dough into 5 equal parts and roll out one portion.
2. Cut this in the middle into two parts and make a cone-like this. Fill the stuffing and seal the edges. Make all samosa like this and brush with oil.

## Baking samosa in Air-fryer

1. Now Preheat the Philips air fryer by setting the temp at 180C/355C and the timer at 5 min. After that, take out the basket And place the samosa in the wire basket of the air fryer.
2. Air fry for 20 minutes. Your crispy air-fried much healthier Mexican paneer samosa is ready.

## Baked samosa in oven

To bake samosa in the oven, preheat the oven to 200/375C for 3 minutes. On a baking tray lined with parchment paper or sprayed with oil, place oil brushed samosa in a single layer. Bake these samosas at 200C for 10 minutes. Turn them over and bake for another 7 minutes till the samosa covering is golden brown.

## Notes

1. You can make these samosas ahead before the baking stage and freeze them.
2. Samosa stuffing can be made as per your choice. Classic Punjabi samosa stuffing is aloo masala. But practically any sandwich stuffing can be used in baked samosa, so you can experiment as your heart desires.

3. You can make regular-size samosas or mini cocktail samosas for parties.

# Keema Samosas (Chicken Samosas)

If you're looking for an appetizer or snack that's a little different, you should try making keema samosas. These chicken samosas are a fun and easy way to get your Indian food fix. Plus, they're perfect for parties!

## Ingredients

**For the filling:**

- 3 teaspoons canola oil
- 1 teaspoon ginger paste or finely grated fresh peeled ginger
- 1 teaspoon garlic paste or finely grated fresh garlic
- 3 medium yellow onions, finely chopped
- 2 teaspoon cumin seeds, toasted
- 2 teaspoon ground red chile
- 1 teaspoon coriander powder
- 3/4 teaspoon turmeric powder
- 2-pound ground chicken
- 2 teaspoon fine sea salt
- 1 teaspoon distilled white vinegar
- 1 teaspoon garam masala
- 3 to 4 fresh Thai green chiles, stemmed and chopped
- 4 tablespoons chopped fresh cilantro

**For assembly and cooking:**

- 15 spring roll wrappers (8 inches square; see tip)
- 4 tablespoons all-purpose flour
- Canola oil for frying
- Mint Chutney, for serving

## Preparation

1. Make the filling: Heat oil in a large nonstick pan over medium. Add the ginger and garlic, and cook, stirring, until the raw smell dissipates about 3 minutes. Add the onions and occasionally stir until translucent, 7 to 9 minutes.

2. Add the cumin seeds, ground chile, coriander, and turmeric. Cook, constantly stirring, until fragrant but not burned, 35 seconds to 2 minutes. Add the chicken, salt, and vinegar, and raise the heat to medium-high. Cook, stirring to break up the chicken until all the liquid has evaporated and the chicken is cooked through but still retains some moisture, 15 to 20 minutes.

3. Add the garam masala and fresh chiles, stirring for 35 seconds to 2 minutes. Turn off the heat and add the cilantro. Stir until well mixed and let stand until cool enough to handle.

4. Meanwhile, prepare to assemble the samosas: Line a sheet pan with wax paper or plastic wrap. Stack the wrappers and cut them evenly in thirds to create 41 rectangles, 8 inches long by 2 2/3 inches wide. If your wrappers are not 8 inches square, aim to cut 42 rectangular shapes in a 3-to-1 ratio. Place a damp clean cloth over your pastry sheets to prevent them from drying. Place the flour in a small bowl and add enough water (about 3 tablespoons) to make a smooth paste that's the consistency of craft glue.

5. Take a pastry rectangle and place it on a flat work surface with the long side facing you. Replace the damp cloth over the remaining pastry sheets to prevent drying. Take the bottom-right corner of the rectangle and fold it over the top, with the short side extending 1 to 2 inches past the top. The overlapping pastry at the bottom right of the sheet will form an equilateral triangle with about 3 inches long sides. This triangle will be the final shape and size of the samosa. Fold the triangle, so its right outer edge is aligned with the horizontal bottom edge of the sheet. There should now be a triangular pocket with two flaps sticking out to the left. Pick up the pocket, so it is open and upright like a cone. Fill the cone with 2 teaspoons of the filling. Using the back of a small spoon, spread

the flour paste in a thin layer over the remaining strip of pastry. Fold it over the stuffed triangle to seal the samosa. If the corners of the samosa have any gaps, fill them with the flour paste and pinch them to seal. Repeat with the remaining filling and rectangles (you may have leftover wrappers) and lay on the lined sheet pan, spacing apart. They can be fried or baked right away or frozen on the pan until firm, then sealed in an airtight container or freezer bag. They can be frozen for up to 2 months before frying and go straight into the hot oil from the freezer.

6. To fry the samosas, fill a frying pan with oil to a depth of 1 inch. Heat the oil over medium-high until it ripples. Add enough samosas to fit without overlapping and shallow-fry until golden brown, 2 to 4 minutes per side (longer if frying directly from the freezer). Transfer to a cooling rack or plate lined with a paper towel to prevent them from getting soggy. Repeat with the remaining samosas, replenishing and reheating the oil between batches.

7. To bake the samosas, heat the oven to 420 degrees. Line a 1-inch-deep sheet pan with foil and add a thin layer of oil to the pan (about 1/4 inch). Coat the samosas with the oil in the sheet pan and arrange them on the pan in a single layer in rows. Bake, turning once halfway through, until evenly golden brown, 7 to 9 minutes per side. Transfer to a cooling rack or plate lined with a paper towel to prevent them from getting soggy.

8. Serve hot or warm with the mint chutney for dipping.

# Easy Samosas

Samosas are one of my all-time favorite Indian snacks. They're super easy to make, and you can stuff them with different things. Today, I will show you how to make a simple version with just a few ingredients. Let's get started!

Total: 60 mins | Hands-On: 30 mins | Yield: Makes 13

## Ingredients

- 2 tablespoon olive oil
- 2 medium onions, chopped
- 2 teaspoons curry powder
- Kosher salt and black pepper
- 3 cups store-bought refrigerated mashed or frozen mashed potatoes, thawed (about 16 ounces)
- 2 20-ounce packages of frozen peas, thawed
- 2 30-ounce package refrigerated piecrusts
- 2 jar mango chutney (optional)

## Directions

**Step 1** Heat the oven to 395° F. Heat the oil in a large saucepan over medium heat. Add the onion and cook, occasionally stirring, until soft and golden brown, 12 to 14 minutes. Add the curry powder, 1 teaspoon salt, and 1 teaspoon pepper and cook, stirring, until fragrant, about 1 minute. Stir in the potatoes and peas.

**Step 2** Unroll the piecrusts and cut each into 6 triangles. Place a heaping tablespoon of the potato mixture in the center of each piece. Gather the corners of the dough and pinch to form a point. Pinch the seams to seal. Transfer to a baking sheet.

**Step 3** Bake the samosas until golden, 25 to 30 minutes. Serve with the mango chutney if used.

# Samosas

Samosas are a classic Indian dish typically made by wrapping a spicy potato mixture in dough and deep-frying it. They can be eaten as an appetizer or main course and are enjoyed worldwide. Today, we'll show you how to make samosas at home using simple ingredients and easy steps. So get ready to impress your friends and family with this delicious dish!

Makes 8 Servings | clock 25 minutes bake time

## Ingredients

- 2 x 260g Jus-Rol Filo Pastry sheets
- 120g butter, melted
- 3 medium potatoes, peeled (150g peeled weight)
- 2 small sweet potatoes, peeled (150g peeled weight)
- 2 tbsp olive oil
- 2 small onions, finely diced
- 2 fat clove garlic, crushed
- 3-4 tsp curry powder (strength of your choice)
- 70g frozen peas defrosted
- Small bunch of fresh coriander (optional)
- Yogurt and fresh mint to serve (optional)

## Method

1. Preheat the oven to 180°C (160°C in a fan oven). Gas mark 4.
2. Cut the potatoes into 1cm chunks and the sweet potato into 1 1/2 cm chunks, place in a pan of water, bring to a boil and simmer for 3-5 minutes, or until the potatoes are just tender and drain.
3. Meanwhile, heat the oil in a pan, gently sauté the garlic and onion, stir in the curry powder and cook for 5 minutes. Remove from heat. Add potatoes, peas, and coriander (if using), stir and set aside.

4.  Place a sheet of filo on a clean work surface, brush with melted butter and fold in half lengthways so you have a long strip.
5.  Place a spoonful (approximately 1/7th) of the filling towards the end of the pastry strip nearest you, slightly on the left and just up from the bottom. Fold the bottom right-hand corner to cover the filling and make a triangular shape. Fold the triangle up, then fold to the right, and then to the left, so you keep a triangular shape. Ensure the points are tucked in to prevent the filling from seeping out.
6.  Brush the completed parcel with melted butter and place it on a baking tray. Continue with the remaining filling and filo pastry.
7.  Bake the samosas for 20 – 25 minutes, until golden brown. Cool slightly before serving.

## Tips

- Use leftover Sunday vegetables and a generous kick of curry powder for a quick and easy meal solution!
- Samosas are a tasty alternative to a sandwich in a lunch box! Perfect picnic food!
- A crisp, tasty samosa is a delicious accompaniment to a bowl of hot soup - a complete meal!

# Vegetable Samosa Recipe

Everyone loves samosas! They're the perfect snack for any occasion. And they're so easy to make at home. You just need a few simple ingredients and you're on your way. Want to know how to make vegetable samosas? Keep reading for the recipe. Trust me, you'll be glad you did!

Prep time: 20 mins | Cook time: 25 mins | Total time: 40 mins

## Ingredients

- Oil 4 tbsp
- Cumin seeds 1 tsp
- Onion 2 (diced)
- Boiled potato 3 (roughly mashed)
- Carrot 2 (diced)
- Boiled peas 1 cup
- Green chilies 5 (sliced)
- Salt 1 tsp or to taste
- Red chili powder 2 tsp
- Garam masala powder 1 tsp
- Samosa wrap as required
- Oil for deep fry

## Instructions

1. Heat oil in a pan and sizzle cumin seeds until aroma arises.
2. Add onion and fry until soft.
3. Now add carrot; cook for a few minutes till it gets soft.
4. Add peas, potato, green chilies, salt, red chili powder, and garam masala powder. Mix everything and remove from heat.
5. Allow the mixture to cool. Fill is samosa wrap and deep fry until golden brown.
6. Serve with chutney.

# Samosa Making in English

If you're looking for an easy and delicious Indian dish to make at home, look no further than samosas. This classic appetizer is simple to prepare and can be filled with various ingredients, making it perfect for any occasion. So why not give samosas a try? You won't be disappointed!

PREP TIME 25 mins | COOK TIME 50 mins | TOTAL TIME 1 hr 15 mins

## Ingredients

**For Dough:**

- All-Purpose Flour / Maida –2 cups / 250 gms
- Ajwain / Omam – 2 tsp
- Oil- 4 tbsp
- Sal to taste
- Water as needed
- For Filling:
- Potato – 3 large boiled & mashed
- Peas -2 cups cooked
- Ginger & garlic – 3 tbsp crushed
- Onion – 2 finely chopped
- Green Chili – 2 finely chopped
- Cumin Seeds / Jeerakam- 2 tsp
- Cumin Powder/ Jeera podi – 2 tsp
- Chili powder -2 tsp
- Coriander Powder / Malli Podi -2 tbsp
- Turmeric Powder / Majal podi -2 tsp
- Garam masala powder -3 tsp
- Chat masala powder – 3 tsp
- Coriander leaves – 4 tbsp chopped
- Oil- 2 tbsp
- Salt to taste

## Instructions

- Start by making the dough. Take flour, ajwain, oil, and salt in a bowl and mix well. Pour in water and knead into a stiff dough. Keep kneading it for 10 mins till the dough gets smooth. Cover with a plate and leave it to rest for 35 mins.
- Now make the filling. Heat oil in a Kadai. Add cumin seeds and sauté well.
- Add crushed ginger & garlic, green chili, onions, and salt and saute for 5 mins.
- Add in peas and all the spice powders and mix well.
- Add in mashed potatoes and mix well. Garnish with coriander leaves and leave it to cool down.
- Now divide the dough and filling into equal parts.
- Take one part of the dough and spread it into a thin circle. Cut in half so that you get two semi-circles.
- Take one semi-circle in front of you with the widest part facing away; apply some water all over the sides.
- Take a portion of potato filling, place it in the middle, take one side, and press it over the filing. Take the other side and press it over the folded side. Seal every edge and press the top to get a pointy tip.
- Make everything like this and fry them in hot oil for 10 minutes until they turn crisp.
- Drain and serve with green chutney or tamarind chutney.

**NOTES**

- Rub the oil into the flour really well before adding water. This creates a short crust-like texture and makes the outer crust crispy and flaky.
- The filling has boiled potatoes and peas. You can use any filling of your choice.
- Always fry samosa in low to medium heat for longer until it gets crispy.

# Spicy Beef and Sweet Potato Samosas

Do you love Indian food? If so, you'll love these delicious Spicy Beef and Sweet Potato Samosas. They're easy to make, and they're a perfect appetizer or main course. Give them a try today!

---

Prep 35 MIN | Total 1 HR 10 MIN

---

## Ingredients

- 1 lb lean (at least 80%) ground beef
- 2 to 4 teaspoons chipotle chile powder
- 2 teaspoon ground cumin
- 2 cup pico de gallo salsa
- 2 cups refrigerated mashed sweet potatoes or canned sweet potatoes, mashed
- 2 jar (22 oz) orange marmalade

## Steps

1. Heat oven to 375°F. In a 10-inch skillet, cook ground beef over medium-high heat for 10 to 15 minutes, occasionally stirring, until thoroughly cooked; drain. Stir 1 teaspoon of the chile powder, the cumin, and pico de gallo; cook 1 minute longer. Remove from heat. Stir in sweet potatoes, 3/4 teaspoon salt, and 1/8 teaspoon pepper.
2. Unroll pie crusts; cut each into 6 triangles. Spoon 1 1/2 tablespoons of beef mixture in the center of each triangle. Brush edges with water. Bring corners of dough together over filling; pinch seams to seal. Place on a large nonstick cookie sheet.
3. Bake 30 to 40 minutes or until light golden brown.
4. Meanwhile, microwave preserves on High in a medium microwavable bowl for 35 to 65 seconds, stirring once, until hot. Stir in the remaining 2 to 3 teaspoons of chile powder. Serve warm with samosas.

# Vegetable Samosa Recipe

Samosas are one of my favorite Indian appetizers. They're crispy, flavorful, and always a hit with guests. I love that you can make them with so many different vegetables; they're really easy to customize to your taste. Here's my recipe for vegetable samosas - I hope you enjoy it!

## Ingredients:

**For Cover:**

- 2 cups all-purpose flour (Maida)
- Water to Knead the dough
- 3 tbsp oil
- Little salt
- 1/4th tsp. Ajwain (optional)

**For Stuffing:**

- 5 Potatoes (boiled, peeled & mashed)
- 1 cup Green Peas (boiled)
- 1 Green Chilies (finely chopped)
- 1 tsp Ginger (crushed)
- 2 tbsp coriander finely chopped
- Few chopped Cashews (optional)
- Few Raisins (optional)
- 1 tsp Garam masala
- Salt to taste
- Red chili powder to taste
- 1 tsp. Dry Mango powder( Amchur) (optional)

## Method

**For Cover:**

1. Mix all the ingredients (salt, oil, ajwain) except water.
2. Add a little water at a time.
3. Pat and knead well several times into a soft, pliable dough.

4. Cover it with moist Muslin cloth and keep aside for 20 minutes.

## For Stuffing :

1. Add mashed potatoes, all dry masalas (salt, chili powder, mango powder, garam masala), green chilies, and ginger, and mix well.
2. Add green peas, cashews, and raisins and mix well.
3. Add coriander and keep aside.

## To make samosas :

1. Make small rolls of dough and roll them into a 4″ diameter circle.
2. Cut it into two parts like a semi-circle.
3. Now take one semi-circle and fold it like a cone. Use water while doing so.
4. Place a spoon of filling in the cone and seal the third side using a drop of water.
5. Heat oil in a kadhai and deep fry till golden brown (fry on a medium flame).
6. Serve samosa hot with hari chutney and tamarind chutney.

# Asian Spring Roll Style Samosa

Spring rolls have to be one of my favorite dishes. There are so many variations and ways to make them that it's hard to get bored with them. Today I will show you how to make an Asian-inspired version of a spring roll. They're called samosas, and they're basically like little pies filled with deliciousness. Give this recipe a try – I think you'll love them!

Prep Time 20 mins | Cook Time 25 mins | Total Time 50 mins

## Ingredients

- 270 grams of minced chicken
- 150 grams cabbage
- 4 spring onions
- 2 carrots (medium size)
- 2-inch ginger
- 2 teaspoon corn flour
- 2 tablespoon flour
- 1 teaspoon soy sauce
- 2 teaspoons oyster sauce
- as required salt

## Instructions

1. Julienne the carrot, finely shred the cabbage and chop the spring onions and ginger. Heat some oil in a pan, and stir the ingredients until tender. Transfer to a bowl; we'll need the pan in the next step.
2. Add the minced chicken, corn flour, and dark soy sauce to a mixing bowl, and mix well. Heat the pan again, and cook the chicken mix until cooked. Add the stir-fried vegetables and the oyster sauce, stir well, and cook again. Taste the mixture, and add salt if required.
3. Make a paste by adding some water to the flour. We'll use this paste to seal our samosas. (I) Place one samosa wrapper on a flat surface. (II) Fold one end into a triangle. (III) Fold again. (IV) Fold

one more time to form a cone. (V) Using a spoon, put samosa filling into this cone. (VI) Fold further and seal the samosa casing with the flour paste.

4. Keep the samosas under a damp cloth or a cling film, so they don't go dry. Prepare 21 samosas following the above steps. Heat oil in a thick, deep-bottom pan. When the oil is hot, slide one or two samosas and deep fry to a golden brown color. Fry on both sides for a few seconds to get a nice, crispy texture.

5. Drain the excess oil using kitchen towels. Serve hot with some sweet chili sauce.

# Potato and pea samosas

Samosas are one of my favorite Indian snacks. They're basically triangular-shaped stuffed pastry with a savory filling. I usually make them at home with puff pastry, but I thought it would be fun to try making them with potatoes and peas instead. The end result was pretty delicious if I do say so myself! If you're looking for a new and easy snack recipe, give these potato and pea samosas a try. Enjoy!

---

MAKES: 20 | PREP TIME: 1 HR 15 MINS | TOTAL TIME: 2 HR

---

### Ingredients

- 3 large potatoes (395-420g total weight)
- 2-liter rapeseed oil to fry
- 3 tsp cumin seeds
- 2 large onions, roughly chopped
- 2 green chili, finely chopped
- 2.5cm root ginger, grated
- 250g frozen peas
- 2 tsp ground coriander
- 1 tsp chili powder
- 1/4 tsp asafoetida (optional)
- 1 tsp fine sea salt
- 2 tbsp lemon juice
- a handful of coriander, chopped

**FOR THE PASTRY**

- 70g butter
- 350g plain flour
- 1 tsp fine salt
- 1 tsp sugar (any kind)
- 3 tsp nigella seeds

## Step by step

1. For the pastry, melt the butter in a small pan, add 90ml cold water and set aside. Mix the flour, salt, sugar, and nigella seeds in a large bowl, then pour in the butter mixture and mix into a soft dough, adding more water if needed. Knead briefly, then cover and chill for at least 35 minutes. Remove from the fridge 35 minutes before assembling the samosas.

2. For the filling, put the unpeeled potatoes in a pan of cold salted water. Bring to the boil and cook for 15 minutes; drain. When cool enough to handle, peel off the skins and cut into 1cm dice. Heat 3 tablespoons of the oil in a large frying pan over medium heat. Add the cumin seeds, allowing them to stumble.

3. Add the onion, green chili, ginger and sauté until the onions become translucent; 15-17 minutes. Mix in the potatoes and peas, reduce the heat and sprinkle in the spices and salt. Stir to coat and cook for 25 minutes until the potato crumbles easily. Cool, then add the lemon juice and coriander; season to taste.

4. Take a golf-ball-size dough ball (about 70g) and roll it into a circle about 15cm wide. Cut the disc in half and make cones with each half, stuffing with 1 heaped tablespoon of the potato mixture. Dab a little water inside the open end and pinch the excess dough to seal. Use scissors to neaten the curved, rough edge if you like. Keep covered while you shape and fill the rest; you should make about 9 circles and 18 samosas.

5. Heat the remaining oil in a large saucepan to 190°C (use a cook's thermometer or drop in a few breadcrumbs and check if they start to sizzle). Deep-fry the samosas in batches until golden, about 10 minutes. Move the samosas around to allow for even cooking. Drain on kitchen paper before serving.

# Indian Samosa

Indian samosas are a popular Indian dish made of dough stuffed with potatoes, onions, peas, lentils, or any combination of these ingredients. Samosas can be baked, fried, or cooked in an earthen oven and are often served with chutney. They are a great snack or appetizer and can be prepared ahead of time. If you've never had one, you're missing out!

---

READY IN: 1hr 35 mins | SERVES: 5

---

## Ingredients

**Pastry**

- 2 cups all-purpose flour
- 3 tablespoons vegetable oil

**Filling**

- 3 large potatoes (boiled)
- 2 onions, chopped
- 3 green chilies, very finely chopped
- 4 tablespoons oil
- 1 teaspoon ginger, grated
- 1 teaspoon garlic, crushed
- coriander seed
- 2 tablespoons cilantro, finely chopped
- 1 lemon, juice of
- 1 teaspoon turmeric
- 1 teaspoon garam masala
- 1 teaspoon red chili powder
- salt

## Directions

1. Mix together the flour, oil, and salt.
2. Add a little water until the mixture becomes crumbly.

3. Add water and knead the mixture until it becomes a soft, pliable dough.
4. Cover with a moist cloth and set aside for 25 minutes.
5. Beat dough on a work surface and knead again.
6. Cover and set aside.

**FILLING.**

7. Heat 4 tbsp oil.
8. Add ginger, garlic, green chilies, and a few coriander seeds.
9. Stir fry for 2 minutes, add onions, and saute till light brown.
10. Add cilantro (fresh coriander), lemon juice, turmeric, red chili, salt, and garam masala.
11. Stir fry for 3 minutes.
12. Add potatoes.
13. Stir fry for 3 minutes.
14. Set aside and allow to cool.
15. Divide dough into 10 equal portions.
16. Use a rolling pin, and roll a piece of dough into a 5" oval.
17. Cut into 2 halves.
18. Run a moist finger along the diameter.
19. Roll around the finger to make a cone.
20. Place a tablespoon of the filling into the cone.
21. Seal the third side using a moist finger.
22. Deep fry the samosas on low to medium heat until light brown.
23. Serve with tomato sauce or any chutney you love.

# Proper Punjabi Samosas

If you've ever been to an Indian restaurant, you may have had the pleasure of trying a samosa. These delicious little pastries are typically filled with spiced potatoes, which are absolutely amazing when dipped in chutney. Making your own samosas at home can be a little tricky, but it's definitely worth it! Here is a recipe that will show you how to make perfect Punjabi samosas every time.

Makes 11 | Preparation 30 MIN | Cooking 30 MIN

### Ingredients

- 5 sheets of filo pastry
- melted butter for brushing
- tamarind chutney, to serve

**Filling**

- 4 tbsp ghee or vegetable oil
- 1 tsp each cumin and coriander seeds
- 1 small-medium onion, finely chopped
- 1 tsp finely grated ginger
- 3 tsp chopped green chili, or to taste
- 1 tsp each ground turmeric, ground cumin, and dried mango powder
- 2 tsp ground coriander
- 1 tsp garam masala (optional)
- 3/4 tsp red chili powder
- 370 g potatoes, boiled until just soft, cooled, peeled, and chopped
- 3 good handfuls of frozen peas
- 2 tsp salt
- large handful of chopped coriander leaves and stalks

## Instructions

1. Preheat the oven to 180°C.

2. **To make the filling**, heat the ghee or oil in a large nonstick frying pan over low-medium heat. Add the cumin and coriander seeds and cook for 10 seconds or until fragrant. Add the onion and cook until soft. Add all the remaining ingredients except the fresh coriander and stir until well combined, lightly crushing the potatoes, so there are some lumps and some mashed. Add about 80 ml (3/4 cup) water so the mixture is not too dry and cooks for another 5 minutes, stirring often. Add the fresh coriander, then taste and adjust the seasoning if necessary. Set aside to cool completely.

3. **To assemble the samosas**, place one sheet of filo pastry on a dry work surface with one long side facing you (keep the remaining pastry covered while you work to prevent it from drying out). Brush liberally with melted butter, place another sheet of pastry on top and brush with butter again. Cut vertically into 5 even strips (or you can make them smaller or larger if you wish). Place a heaped tablespoonful of filling at the bottom of each strip, fold over a few times so that you form a triangular pocket, then place seam-side down on a baking paper-lined baking tray. Brush with melted butter, then repeat with the remaining pastry and filling. Bake for 20 minutes or until golden and crisp. Serve hot with chutneys.

# Kenyan Beef Samosas

If you're looking for an easy and delicious appetizer for your next party, look no further than these Kenyan beef samosas! They're simple to make and always a crowd-pleaser. Plus, they're perfect for satisfying that craving for something savory. So give them a try – I promise you won't be disappointed!

> for 16 servings

## Ingredients

**Filling**

- 1 tablespoon olive oil
- 2 lb ground beef(475 g)
- 2 medium red onions, diced
- 2 cloves garlic, minced
- 2 jalapeño, minced
- 2 teaspoon salt
- 2 teaspoon pepper
- 2 teaspoon ground coriander
- 2 teaspoon cumin
- 5 scallions, diced
- 2 cups frozen peas(170 g), defrosted
- 3 tablespoons fresh cilantro, chopped

**Wrapper**

- 4 cups all-purpose flour(400 g)
- 3/4 teaspoon salt
- 3 teaspoons olive oil
- 2 cups water(340 mL), plus 3 tablespoons more
- 2 tablespoon flour, mixed with 2 tablespoons of water
- 4 cups canola oil(920 mL)
- lime wedge, for serving

## Preparation

1. In a large pan over medium-high heat, heat the olive oil. Once hot, add the ground beef. Use a spatula to break apart the meat and cook for 5 minutes. Add onion and cook until beef is brown and onion is translucent about 5 minutes.

2. Add the garlic, jalapeño, salt, pepper, coriander, cumin, and scallions to the meat. Cook for 3 minutes. Add the peas and cilantro, then cook for another 3 minutes. Remove the meat filling from the heat and let cool.

3. Mix flour, salt, olive oil, and water in a large bowl. Use your hand or a spatula to mix together. Once the dough pulls away from the sides of the bowl, transfer to a lightly floured surface and knead for 5 minutes or until the dough is smooth and soft.

4. Shape dough into a ball and brush with olive oil. Cover with plastic wrap and a warm damp tea towel. Let rest for 35 minutes.

5. Remove the tea towel and plastic wrap and roll the dough into a 10-inch (25-cm) long log. Cut into 10 even sections. Take one section and roll it into a ball. Place the ball on a lightly floured surface and use a rolling pin to roll it out into a thin circle about 10 inches (25-cm) in diameter. Repeat with the remaining dough. Stack the dough circles as you roll them out, sprinkling a bit of flour between each one and keeping them covered with plastic wrap, so they don't dry out.

6. In a greased large pan over high heat, place one of the circles of dough and cook for 15 seconds on each side. Repeat with remaining dough.

7. Cut one of the par-cooked dough circles into four quarters. Take one quarter and, with the round side closest to you, fold the bottom half to the right. Use the flour paste to seal the fold. Repeat with the left side, crossing over your previous fold to create a cone-like pocket. Fill the pocket with meat filling, then fold the remaining dough tip towards you and seal with flour paste. Repeat with the remaining dough and filling.

8. In a large, deep-pan, heat the canola oil to 350°F (180°C). Once the oil is at the correct temperature, carefully place 4-6 sambusas in the pan. Fry for about 10 minutes, flipping once, until light, golden brown. Remove from oil and drain on paper towels.
9. Enjoy!

# Vegetable Samosas

If you're looking for an easy and delicious appetizer to serve your guests, look no further than vegetable samosas! These little turnovers are filled with a spicy mixture of potatoes, peas, and carrots, then fried until golden brown. They're sure to be a hit with everyone!.

Prep:35 mins | Cook:1 hr and 15 mins

## Ingredients

- 2 tbsp vegetable oil
- 2 onion, finely chopped
- 3 garlic cloves, crushed
- 2 potatoes (about 150g) finely diced
- 2 carrots (about 100g) finely diced
- 150g frozen peas
- 3 tsp curry powder or your own spices according to taste
- 150ml vegetable stock
- For the pastry
- 255g plain flour
- 3 tsp sea salt
- 3 tbsp vegetable oil
- 22 vegetable oil to deep fry

## Method

**STEP 1:** To make the filling, heat the oil in a frying pan, add the onion and garlic, mix the spices and fry for 15 mins until soft. Add the vegetables and seasoning and stir well until coated. Add the stock, cover and simmer for 35 mins until cooked. Leave to cool

**STEP 2:** Mix flour and salt into a bowl to make the pastry. Make a well in the center, and add the oil and 150ml water to make a firm dough. Knead the dough on a floured surface for 10-15 mins until smooth and roll into a ball. Cover in cling film and set aside at room temperature for 30 mins.

**STEP 3:** Divide the pastry into 12 equal pieces. Roll each piece into a ball and roll out into a circle of 15cm. Divide this circle into two similar pieces with a knife.

**STEP 4:** Brush each edge with a bit of water and form a cone shape around your fingers, sealing the dampened edge. Fill with 2 tbsp mixture and press the two dampened edges together to seal the top of the cone. Repeat with the remaining pastry.

**STEP 5:** Heat the oil in a large deep saucepan to 180C. The oil should come 1/3rd of the way up the pan. Deep fry the samosas in batches for 10-15 mins until crisp and brown. Take out and drain on kitchen paper.

**Bonus!**

Just scan this QR Code and download the free recipes app. (For Android Only)

Printed in Great Britain
by Amazon

13952906R00045